# PITTSBUI

# HISTOF

# BALLPARKS

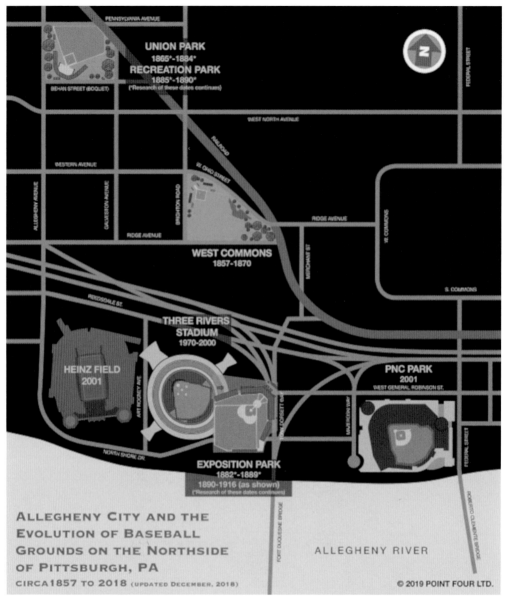

ALLEGHENY CITY AND THE
EVOLUTION OF BASEBALL
GROUNDS ON THE NORTHSIDE
OF PITTSBURGH, PA

ALLEGHENY RIVER

CIRCA1857 TO 2018 (UPDATED DECEMBER, 2018)

© 2019 POINT FOUR LTD.

This map shows the Northside location of five of the region's major ballparks, from the earliest documented local ball field in 1857 to today's PNC Park. All are within blocks of each other, making this area the cradle of baseball in Pittsburgh. (Courtesy of Point Four Ltd.)

FRONT COVER: The epicenter of Pittsburgh baseball for 61 years was the main entrance to Forbes Field, seen here in 1909, the park's first season. (Courtesy of Library of Congress.)

COVER BACKGROUND: Pittsburgh's Northside was home to the earliest ballparks, including Exposition Park. In 1970, baseball returned to the Northside, nearly on the same site as the Old Ball Grounds. (Courtesy of Library of Congress.)

BACK COVER: Pirates hitters, including a young Roberto Clemente, take aim at a pennant in front of the Forbes Field dugout. (Courtesy of Pittsburgh Pirates Archives.)

# PITTSBURGH'S HISTORIC BALLPARKS

*Mark T. Fatla*

ARCADIA
PUBLISHING

Published by Arcadia Publishing
Charleston, South Carolina

Printed in the United States of America

Library of Congress Control Number: 2022948573

For all general information, please contact Arcadia Publishing:
Telephone 843-853-2070
Fax 843-853-0044
E-mail sales@arcadiapublishing.com
For customer service and orders:
Toll-Free 1-888-313-2665

Visit us on the Internet at www.arcadiapublishing.com

*This book is dedicated to my patient wife, Elaine, and to my mother, Genevieve, a lifelong Pirates fan who shook the Green Weenie and brought the Babushka Power!*

# CONTENTS

# ACKNOWLEDGMENTS

In 1986, my wife and I bought an 1870 house in a Northside historic district, a mere five blocks from Three Rivers Stadium. Walking to Pirates games, I wondered how the fans who lived in my house in the Victorian era experienced Recreation Park or Exposition Park.

This book began with the pandemic, leaving me dependent on the kindness of many people in very difficult times. Martin Aurand of Carnegie Mellon University's Architecture Archives was the first to respond with rare images of Greenlee Field. Bruce Klein of Photo Antiquities Museum of Photography quickly provided unpublished photographs of Forbes Field. Donna Williams graciously provided family history and documentation on her grandfather's nearly forgotten Central Park and the Pittsburgh Keystones. David Stinson of Deadballbaseball.com provided rare photographs of West Field.

Local baseball historians Andy Terrick and Len Martin provided leads, encouragement, and editing for historical accuracy. This book would not have been possible without their knowledge and their kindness. Any errors that remain are mine alone.

I owe the greatest debts to Dan Hart of the Pittsburgh Pirates and David Grinnell of the University of Pittsburgh Archives. Both were generous with their images, time, and good cheer despite the disruptions of the pandemic. Patient technical help was provided by Lauren Stauffer, who helped overcome my considerable deficiencies with technology. My sincerest thanks, as well, go to Jim Plake of the Pirates, Jimmy Sacco of the Steelers, coach Dan McCann of Duquesne University, and various representatives from the following (with a key to photograph credits): Brookline Library (BL), Carnegie Museum of Art (CMOA), Carnegie Mellon University Architecture Archives (CMUAA), Deadball Baseball (DB), Heinz History Center (HHC), Library of Congress (LOC), Pittsburgh Pirates Archives (PP), Pittsburgh Steelers Archives (PS), Point Four Ltd. / Len Martin (PF), Rivers of Steel Heritage Corp (ROS), University of Pittsburgh Archives (UP), and Williams Family Archives (WFA). Please note that AC denotes images from the author's collection.

# INTRODUCTION

Pittsburgh has been home to some of baseball's greatest players. Honus Wagner was one of the first five men inducted into the National Baseball Hall of Fame and is still regarded by many as the greatest shortstop in baseball history. Northside resident Josh Gibson, forced to play on the wrong side of baseball's color line, became the most feared slugger in the Negro Leagues, standing, in the eyes of many, on equal footing with Babe Ruth. Roberto Clemente thrilled a generation with his grace, skill, and passion and, in his last act, filled a nation with grief at his untimely passing, and admiration for his unselfish philanthropy that lives on in Major League Baseball's annual Clemente Award for community service. Willie Stargell reminded everyone that baseball is a joy, not a job, and showed how a diverse collection of men could become not just a team but also a "Fam-A-Lee." Along the way, Fred Clarke, Arky Vaughn, Pie Traynor, Kiki Cuyler, Paul and Lloyd Waner, Ralph Kiner, Bill Mazeroski, and others carved out hall-of-fame careers.

Great teams graced these ballparks, giving Pittsburgh a rich sports tradition. The Pirates of 1900 to 1909 won four National League pennants and the 1909 World Series. The Pirates teams of the 1920s played an exciting brand of baseball and won a World Series in 1925, then bowed to the 1927 "Murderers Row" New York Yankees of Babe Ruth, Lou Gehrig, and a new style of play that prized sluggers and the home run. The Pittsburgh Crawfords and Homestead Grays produced multiple championships and gave Pittsburgh a Negro League tradition that is unequaled. The "Beat 'em Bucs" of 1960, Clemente's 1971 champions, and the "We Are Fam-A-Lee" Pirates of 1979 brought more thrills to Pittsburgh's ballparks. Also along the way, the Pittsburgh Steelers, the University of Pittsburgh's Pitt Panthers, and Duquesne University's Iron Dukes played out championship football seasons on the turf of these venues.

Pittsburgh has also known some of baseball's greatest moments. In 1903, the first modern World Series, matching Barney Dreyfuss's Pirates against the Boston Americans (later "Red Sox"), paved the way for peace between the National and American Leagues and the basic structure of Major League Baseball that survives to the present. In 1925, Kiki Cuyler's two-run double off of Washington Senators great Walter Johnson in the bottom of the eighth inning of game seven made the Pirates the first team to come back from a 3-1 deficit to win the World Series. In 1971, Pirates manager Danny Murtaugh quietly made history by fielding the first all-minority lineup, led by Roberto Clemente. Nothing tops October 13, 1960, when Bill Mazeroski stepped to the plate at Forbes Field in the bottom of the ninth inning in a tie game and launched himself into history with the quintessential walk-off home run, a feat still celebrated annually in front of the remains of the Forbes Field wall.

But while most baseball fans know these great players, teams, and moments, the stories of their ballparks are largely forgotten. Forbes Field has attracted an almost mythic nostalgic status that obscures its long and varied history. Three Rivers Stadium, like many of the cookie-cutter concrete bowls of the 1960s and 1970s, is often reviled; though, championships by the Pirates and

Steelers redeem it in the minds of those willing to overlook the architecture for the performances on the field. While some fans may have heard of Exposition Park, few know the earlier Union Park and Recreation Park, and the history of Pittsburgh's Negro League parks has been literally wiped off the landscape.

This is particularly surprising because Pittsburgh has long been a national leader in ballpark development. Exposition Park was regarded as one of the finest of the Victorian-era wooden parks. Forbes Field and Philadelphia's Shibe Park opened within weeks of each other in 1909 and kicked off a steel-and-concrete building wave in baseball. Forbes Field would survive 61 years as one of the first, best, and longest lived of the "modern" parks. In the Negro Leagues, the nearly forgotten Central Amusement Park, or Central Park for short, became in 1921 the first ballpark in the nation owned, designed, and built by African Americans. Just 12 years later, the same architect designed Greenlee Field for black businessman and numbers kingpin Gus Greenlee and his white partners. For seven seasons in the 1930s, Greenlee Field would host the Pittsburgh Crawfords and, on occasion, the Homestead Grays, along with boxing matches, auto races, and practice sessions of Art Rooney's Pittsburgh Pirates football team, later renamed the Steelers.

Though it was not the first of its kind, Three Rivers Stadium was emblematic of the multiuse concrete bowl era of the 1960s and 1970s and, perhaps, the most successful. Over its 30 year life, the Pirates and Steelers teams that called it home gave Pittsburgh the nickname "City of Champions." Unlike Forbes Field's long and painful demolition, Three Rivers Stadium went in an instant, demolished in a controlled implosion by the flick of a switch. PNC Park arose just across the parking lots from the rubble of Three Rivers Stadium, and today, it is widely acclaimed as the best of the retro-park design movement. Its riverfront location with a view of Pittsburgh's downtown evokes vague memories of Exposition Park a century earlier with its similar location and dramatic view of the city across the Allegheny River.

The goal of this book is to tell the story of ballpark development in Pittsburgh. Photographs chronicle design and construction phases, the major changes as parks expanded and aged, and eventually their demolition. Here also are the monuments and the surrounding area that became part of the fan experience. The great players, teams, and moments are not the focus. There are many other books to tell their stories. Here, those players, teams, and moments are seen only as they illustrate the look and condition of the ballparks themselves.

A wide variety of sources was searched for photographs to illustrate this history, including team archives, museums, newspapers, and private collections. Included are rarely seen images and several that have never been published, most notably the only known image of Central Park, home of the 1921–1922 Pittsburgh Keystones of the Negro National League. It was discovered just prior to publication. More images of the parks continue to become available and will fill in gaps in the story of their development, or correct any mistakes inadvertently made in this book.

You may know the stories of Pittsburgh's star players and championship teams, but this is the story of the ballparks where baseball's great moments unfolded.

# BEGINNINGS
## UNION PARK AND
## RECREATION PARK

The earliest documented baseball game in the area was played in 1857 in the West Commons in Pittsburgh's sister city of Allegheny, now the Northside. Like many cities, Pittsburgh saw a surge of interest in baseball as soldiers returned from the Civil War, having learned the game to pass the time in camp. Union Park in the city of Allegheny began as a skating rink and advertised "Base Ball on the Ice!" for Christmas Day 1865. The grounds were soon adapted in good weather months to host real games by the growing number of amateur baseball teams.

In 1876, the first local professional team, the Allegheny, leased Union Park for its home games. In 1877, the team joined the International Association, an early rival to the newly formed National League. The team played well, finishing second with 13 wins and 6 losses, but folded 12 games into its second season, winning just once. The team reorganized and played as an independent team, playing for money and competition rather than a championship trophy. The Indianapolis Blues of the National League, drawing poorly at home, relocated to Union Park temporarily for several games in 1877, playing the first National League games in Pittsburgh.

At first, fans stood along the foul lines or sat in the grass at Union Park. Gradually, benches and open-air bleachers were added. In May 1876, a roofed pavilion was built behind home to seat 300 to 500 fans, and a 12-foot fence enclosed the grounds. Wooden construction was rudimentary, if not shoddy. Two months later, a storm blew down the pavilion and sections of fence.

In 1882, a new club with the Allegheny name joined the American Association and built a grandstand on the Exposition Grounds near the river. Flooding and storm damage made that site problematic, and by 1884, the team returned to Union Park, building a new grandstand to accommodate 2,500 fans. The next year, with grand plans to also host concerts, plays, and other events, they renamed it Recreation Park. Pittsburgh's first real ballpark was taking shape.

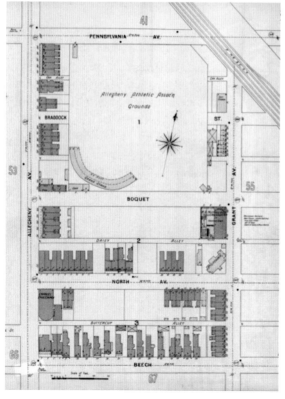

The location of Pittsburgh's earliest documented ball field in the West Commons at Brighton Road and Western Avenue has been superimposed on this modern aerial photograph. Other than the basic orientation of the field, details are speculative. PNC Park stands at top center and the site of Exposition Park is to its right. The author's home is just out of the shot at the bottom of the image. (PF.)

Union Park developed just blocks from the 1857 ball field. By 1884, a new grandstand was constructed, and in 1885, it was renamed Recreation Park. As seen in this insurance map of the era, the park was in the prosperous and growing city of Allegheny, across the river from Pittsburgh. In the winter, the site housed an ice-skating pond and a toboggan slide. (UP.)

Born in Pittsburgh in 1847, Al Pratt, pictured standing at center, was a Civil War veteran and early professional ballplayer. He is shown here with Forest City, the first professional team in Cleveland. In 1880, he founded and managed the Allegheny team in his home town. Known in later years as "Uncle Al," Pratt was an honored guest at Pittsburgh baseball events until 1937, when he passed at age 90. (AC.)

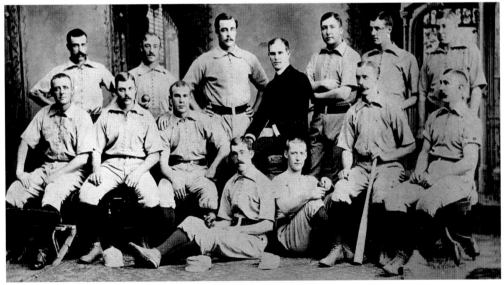

The 1885 Alleghenys were the first to use the renamed Recreation Park. They finished a respectable third in the eight-team American Association and rose to second in 1886. The grandstand featured 2,000 orchestra chairs, private boxes, an owner's box, and press box. With a good team and a handsome park, attendance was strong (PP.)

With a successful 1886 season, the Alleghenys shifted to the National League for 1887. This newspaper advertisement promoted the inaugural game in the league. Typical of season openers and other big games of the era are the parade, band concert, and speeches by local dignitaries. Rain delayed the game to April 30. Although the franchise began in 1882, the current Pittsburgh Pirates date their history to this game. (*Pittsburgh Post.*)

The 1887 team began Pittsburgh's tenure in the National League. They are posed in front of the Recreation Park grandstand with fans behind. This Kalamazoo Bats tobacco card is one of the rarest early baseball cards—only four have been found to date. (PP)

PITTSBURG B. B. C.

Two future hall of famers played the 1887 season with Recreation Park as their home field but under radically different circumstances. Pud Galvin of the Alleghenys was one of the dominant major-league pitchers of the era, the first to reach the 300-win plateau. He is seen here on a period tobacco card. (LOC.)

King Solomon "Sol" White was a 19-year-old infielder on the first Negro League team in the region, the Keystones. The Keystones also called Recreation Park home, but baseball's color line prevented Galvin and White from facing each other. White had a long career as a player, manager, and executive, and wrote an important early history of black baseball. (LOC.)

Recreation Park is home to a ballpark legend. Alleghenys star Fred Carroll, seen here in a vintage baseball card, owned a monkey that doubled as team mascot. The monkey died, and the legend claims Carroll buried it under home plate on the eve of the team's inaugural National League game in 1887. Local historians doubt the tale, and a warehouse now occupies the site, precluding an exploratory dig. (LOC.)

The 1889 team is posed in front of the Recreation Park grandstand. Galvin is seated at far left in the second row. Unlike fixed stadium seats that came into vogue later, the front rows consist of individual chairs. This style of seating continued up to the creation of Forbes Field. (PP.)

The surrounding hills provided vantage points, though at a distance, for fans to watch the games for free. In 1889, a reporter used a telescope to write a game account. This sketch from the article shows the view from the hill—a double-deck grandstand with bleachers along the base lines. (*Pittsburgh Dispatch*.)

HOW THE INGLORIOUS DEFEAT APPEARED FROM OBSERVATORY HILL—MORE PICTURESQUE THAN PRACTICAL.

AT THE BALL GROUNDS.

An 1889 news article described how reporters covered games at the ballpark. It included this rare sketch of the press box on the second tier of the grandstand. Note that the rear wall ends short of the roof, allowing air circulation in the summer heat. When the Alleghenys moved to Exposition III in 1891, the Allegheny Athletic Association took control, and the field became known as 3A Park. (*Pittsburgh Press*.)

Recreation Park was also home for the growing sport of football. In 1892, the Allegheny Athletic Association and Pittsburgh Athletic Association were scheduled to play. Both teams sought help from college star William "Pudge" Heffelfinger. Allegheny won the bidding and the game. Pudge caused and recovered a fumble for the game's only touchdown. The club's ledger included Pudge's $500 fee—the first documentation of payment to a player. (AC.)

This c. 1894 grainy cyanotype is the only known photograph of the grandstand at Recreation Park. It was discovered in 2015 in the cornerstone of a demolished building on the hill overlooking the site of the park. In the foreground at right is part of the Allegheny Observatory. In the valley below is Recreation Park, a mature and substantial wooden park of the Victorian era. (HHC.)

Though the Alleghenys moved to Exposition Park in 1891, Recreation Park's location adjacent to a rail line made it popular for carnivals, traveling circuses, amateur baseball, and other attractions. This 1894 newspaper illustration shows the grandstand with a track for cycle racing. (*Pittsburgh Press*.)

Recreation Park was an early home of the football team of the Western University of Pennsylvania, later renamed the University of Pittsburgh. This 1899 team photograph was taken in the infield grass looking out to center field. The outfield fence is visible at left. The team eventually moved full time to Exposition Park, and the grandstand that saw the Alleghenys play was dismantled. (UP.)

Bosses of Pittsburgh Club 190?- 5.

In 1901, Barney Dreyfuss leased Recreation Park to block the new American League from competing in Pittsburgh. He erected a cycling track, renamed the "Coliseum" or "Colosseum." Dreyfuss now had experience with two wooden ballparks and began formulating the vision that would become Forbes Field. Here, he is seated in his office with team officers and a trophy commemorating the 1901 National League pennant. (PP.)

This 1902 newspaper photograph of a Western University of Pennsylvania game provides a grainy but rare glimpse of the later grandstand. Having brokered peace with the American League, Dreyfuss gave up his lease in 1904. In 1910, newspapers reported sale of the land to a new outlaw baseball league, but it fizzled before playing a game. Industrial uses replaced the field, and Recreation Park faded from memory. (*Pittsburgh Dispatch.*)

# WOODEN GEM

## EXPOSITION PARK, 1890–1909

The Exposition Buildings, akin to a modern convention center, opened in Allegheny City in 1875 to promote the region's industry, innovation, and pride. The broad flat land between the Exposition Buildings and the Allegheny River quickly took the name Exposition Grounds. The first improvement for sports was the creation of an oval track for horse racing.

In 1882, the Alleghenys joined the American Association, an early major league, and erected a grandstand on the Exposition Grounds (Exposition I). During that first season, the grounds were in such poor condition from flooding that the team considered moving to Union Park but stuck it out.

For the 1883 season, the Alleghenys erected a new grandstand west of Exposition I, roughly on the present site of Heinz Field. But this field (Exposition II) flooded as well, and by June 12, the team returned to Exposition I. The team had now invested in two grandstands, but repeated flooding was rendering those investments useless. For 1884, the team returned to Union Park and built what became known as Recreation Park in 1885.

With the Exposition Grounds vacant, the struggling Chicago Browns of the new Union Association baseball league moved mid-season in 1884 to become the Pittsburgh Stogies. The move did not help. The team soon folded, and so did the Union Association.

For the rest of the 1880s, the Exposition Grounds were in active use but without Major League Baseball. In 1890, that changed dramatically. Players had chafed for years under control of the owners, enduring salary caps, unilateral and unappealable fines and discipline, and the near servitude of the reserve clause. Players organized an early union, the Brotherhood of Professional Ballplayers, and when owners would not accommodate player concerns, the union found investors and created the Players League in 1890.

The Brotherhood of Professional Ballplayers attracted many star players from the National League and American Association, and their investors developed new ballparks or refurbished old ones. In Pittsburgh, the Exposition Grounds were leased, and a new ballpark was built (Exposition III). Like its predecessors, it would be plagued by flooding but it would host Major League Baseball for 25 years.

Here are the Exposition Grounds with the racetrack oval and grandstand. The pyramidal roofed stairwells that became a defining element of Exposition III are seen on the older grandstand. Whether the Alleghenies played in front of this grandstand or built another is unclear, but repeated flooding in 1882–1883 chased them back to Union Park. (BL.)

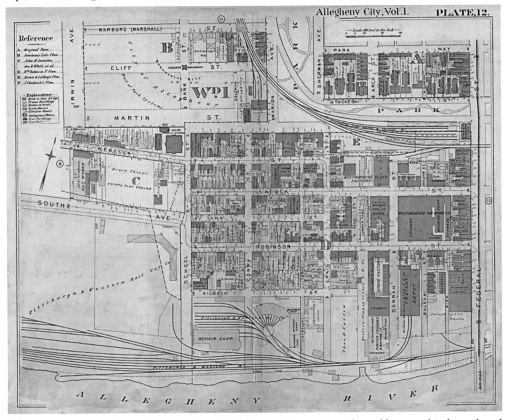

This insurance map shows the footprint of the Players League grandstand hemmed in by railroad lines and a densely packed neighborhood in close proximity to the Allegheny River. The Civil War Soldiers Monument, seen in many photographs of the park, is noted at the top of the map. (UP.)

The 1896 Pirates pose in front of the grandstand with box seat chairs visible. Second baseman Louis Bierbauer is third from left in the third row. The Alleghenys signed Bierbauer to a contract following the collapse of the 1890 Players League. His previous team in Philadelphia objected, labeling the signing "piratical." Pittsburgh eagerly embraced the "Pirates" identity. The slender fellow at center in the second row is player/manager Connie Mack. (LOC.)

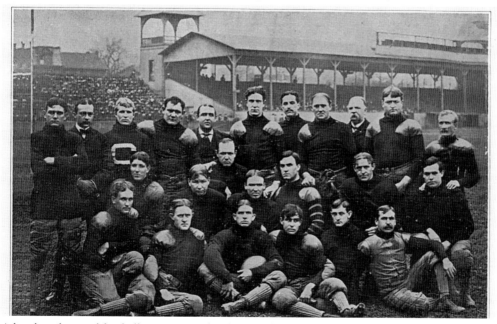

A local professional football team is posed in front of the first base side of the grandstand, providing a view of the park in 1899, just before Barney Dreyfuss acquired the Pirates. The pyramid roof on the staircase tower is plainly seen, as are the original rooftop boxes. (Pittsburgh Bulletin.)

The team's fortunes changed dramatically in 1900 when the National League contracted from 12 teams to 8, and Barney Dreyfuss transferred the best of his Louisville club to Pittsburgh. Here is Exposition Park as it appeared on Opening Day, April 26, 1900. It already enjoyed a reputation as one of the finest ballparks of its time, and Dreyfuss would reinvest in his facility over the coming years. The symmetrical grandstand and flanking bleachers are packed. The twin stair towers are

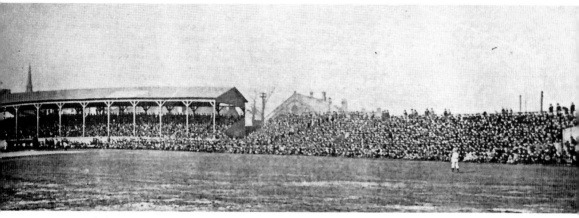

prominent behind the grandstand. The rooftop boxes only occupy a small stretch behind home. This view from deep center gives an impression of a spacious outfield, and Exposition was indeed a difficult place to clear the fences. One player capable of that kind of slugging was a young shortstop from Carnegie, Pennsylvania, Honus "Hans" Wagner. (UP.)

This photograph from Opening Day 1900 gives a close-up view of the grandstand with its trident bracing and the distinctive roof of the east staircase. The roof box at top left is the press box. A screen tops it to prevent fouls from leaving the park. The dugout is tiny, but rosters of that era usually consisted of 16 active players (UP.)

From the field directly behind home, the wood plank facade of the grandstand is clear. The floor of the front row of the stands was only three or four feet above field level. The banner visible in the stands at right is for Pickering's, a local furniture and home goods store. It is being held up by two men in an early effort at ballpark advertising! (UP.)

Players warm up on Opening Day 1900. Wire screening is visible at left, and the dugout is crowded. For the first time in 10 years, the local "cranks" would see a top-notch ball club. The Pirates would finish second in 1900, then win the National League pennant in 1901, 1902, and 1903, and play the first modern World Series at Exposition in 1903. (UP.)

The bleachers on Opening Day, April 26, 1900, are packed shoulder to shoulder with men in bowler hats and a few boys. Not a single woman is visible. A Pittsburgh policeman stands to keep order. The fans got their money's worth. The Pirates battled but dropped a thriller to the Cincinnati Reds 12-11. (UP.)

Exposition hosted the first modern World Series in 1903 against Boston. Compare this image with the 1900 photograph. This view from the seats on the first base side shows the rooftop boxes have been extended the full length of the grandstand, and every seat is filled. Dreyfuss reinvested in his facility to increase his financial return, a pattern repeated at Forbes Field. (PP.)

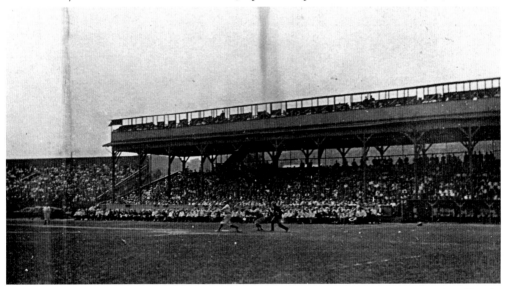

This undated photograph shows seating added on the field in front of the grandstand. Ballparks were not prepared for the explosive growth of baseball in the early 1900s, and such temporary solutions were common. (PP.)

The team raised its National League championship pennant on Opening Day, April 21, 1904. The flagpole is in play in deep center field. Billboards, the covered wooden Union Bridge, Mount Washington, and Pittsburgh's smoky atmosphere are all plainly visible. (BL.)

After raising its pennant, the team returns to the dugout, led by a brass band. The scoreboard is on the right field wall. Unlike the smooth arc of most infields, the outer grass edge pinches in behind second base, creating a somewhat heart-shaped infield. This unique feature would soon disappear. (BL.)

By 1903, Dreyfuss had a successful club in a fine wooden park, and by helping to broker peace with the American League, he had emerged as a leading figure in baseball. Here he is posed in front of the first base grandstand and the bleachers along the right field line. The rooftop boxes extend the full length of the grandstand. (PP.)

Big games on holidays and pennant races brought huge crowds, like this August 23, 1904, doubleheader against the rival New York Giants. When the stands were filled, ropes were strung in the outfield, and standing tickets were sold. A sloped terrace rose up from the field to the outfield fence, giving some standees a view over the heads of the folks at the rope. (LOC.)

The 1905 Pirates pose in front of the empty Exposition Park grandstand and left field bleachers. Honus Wagner is second from right. He would play until 1917, manage the team for five games in 1917, serve as a much-loved coach from 1933 to 1952, and be memorialized in a bronze statue in 1955. He is still regarded by many as the greatest shortstop to play the game. (LOC.)

Another undated photograph shows game action with packed right field bleachers. As a reminder that the riverfronts were largely industrial in that era, looming over the bleachers in the distant gray mist is a tall cylindrical structure. This was a storage tank that would expand as it was filled with natural gas. In 1927 at that location, three such tanks exploded, killing 26 people and damaging buildings for miles. (BL.)

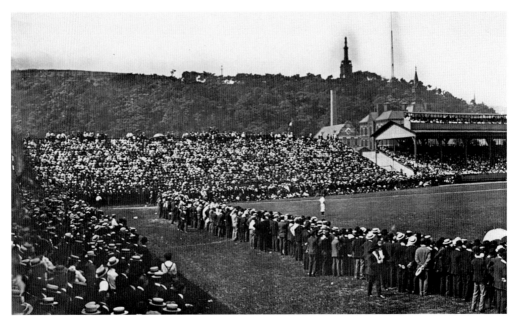

The four images on these two pages form a long panorama of a game against the New York Giants on August 5, 1905, in the heat of a pennant race. Attendance was a ballpark record of 18,383, which included fans standing behind ropes in the outfield and on temporary bleachers, seen here in the first panel on the right field side. Looming above the park is the Civil War Soldiers Monument. (LOC.)

The second panel of the panorama shows the grandstand from center field. Games drew a largely male fan base, though some women are visible. The Pirates and Giants battled to a 5-5 tie until Giants manager John McGraw disputed an umpire's call and pulled his team off the field, forfeiting the game to the Pirates. (LOC.)

The third panel shows the left field line bleachers with additional seating on the field in front of them, plus temporary bleachers against the left field wall and an army of standees. Fans are even standing atop the fence to get a view of the game. (LOC.)

Completing the panorama is a view of the left field bleachers and the outfield wall. Whiskey advertisements reflect the mostly male fan base. More fans have climbed to the tops of the walls rather than be shut out of the big game. (LOC.)

This undated view shows the right field fence with more whiskey advertisements and, most notably, the hand-operated scoreboard at right. Beyond the fence, railcars and the covered wooden Union Bridge are visible. The bridge would be badly damaged in a flood in 1907, severing an important link to Pittsburgh and motivating the Pirates to build Forbes Field. (PP.)

This undated view is from high in the right field bleachers, across the infield to the opposite bleachers. This was clearly a big game, with fans standing on the field along the left field line in front of the bleachers. The infield now has a more conventional circular edge. (PP.)

PNC Park boasts spectacular views of Downtown Pittsburgh, but Exposition beat PNC by a century. This view of the left field bleachers shows the city just across the river. The building under construction at far left with the central light well is the Fulton Building, built in 1906, thereby dating this photograph. The Fulton survives today as the Renaissance Pittsburgh Hotel and is visible from PNC Park. (PP.)

Typical of the time, fans exited the park by crossing the field, especially those standing at the edge of the outfield during big games. This undated photograph from the right field bleachers shows the free-for-all as fans race for the exits to crowd onto the streetcars. (PP.)

Another undated view from a big game shows a real mass of humanity on the field following a game. Note the side of the rooftop boxes at top left. They look to be only three rows deep. This feature would be adopted and expanded as part of the design of Forbes Field. (PP.)

This view outside the 1B side of the park along South Street shows an exterior fence covered with advertising signs. Despite the revenue from the signs, owner Barney Dreyfuss would ban them at Forbes Field, preferring a classier look without billboards. The distinctive stair towers are at left. (BL.)

Exposition's location near the Allegheny River made flooding a regular occurrence, and ultimately doomed it. Rowboats were not unusual in such events. This view is from General Robinson Street to the 3B stair tower. (AC.)

ALONG WATER STREET, PITTSBURG. FOUR SQUARES FROM JUNCTION OF THE ALLEGHENY AND MONONGAHELA.

BOATING AT THE ENTRANCE TO BASE BALL PARK, ALLEGHENY.

Greatest flood ever recorded in Allegheny county, Mononaghela river guaging 36.2 ft. of water, and Allegheny river 36.6 ft. Next greatest flood, the celebrated "Pumpkin Flood" of 1832, followed by the 1884 flood, which was 3.3 ft. less.

The 1907 flood was marked by this postcard showing the main entrance building behind home plate, at the intersection of School (later Scotland) and South Streets. This flood was catastrophic for the team, damaging the Union Bridge so badly that it was demolished, severing a major link between the ballpark and its fans across the river in Pittsburgh. (AC.)

This panorama from deep down the right field line shows the park on July 2, 1908. The pyramid roofs have been removed, eliminating a defining feature of the park. In addition to regular flooding, wooden parks like Exposition were constantly in danger of destruction by fire. In a later news article, the Pirates longtime facilities manager described how staff would climb under the

stands after games, looking for smoldering cigars among the discarded ticket stubs and programs. Dreyfuss had been looking for solutions to these twin problems of water and fire. In less than a year, the Pirates would abandon Exposition for their grand concrete-and-steel masterpiece, Forbes Field. (LOC.)

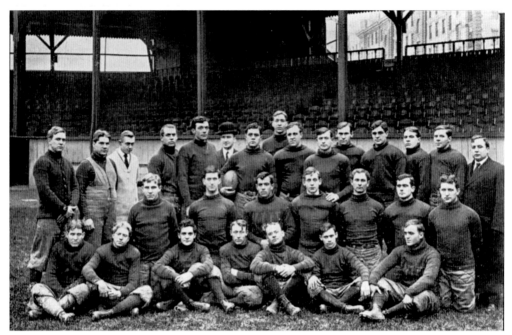

Exposition Park also hosted football games, including serving as the home field of the Western University of Pennsylvania from 1900 to 1908, when the college was renamed the University of Pittsburgh. This 1907 team photograph from the *Owl* yearbook provides a view of the grandstand's interior. (UP.)

The 1908 Pitt team finished 8-3, including a 22-0 win in the November 3 game against Carnegie Tech. Pitt's 1908 team was the first college team to wear uniform numbers, visible in this postcard. The third base grandstand, rooftop boxes, and left field line bleachers are all in view. Pitt followed the Pirates to Forbes Field in 1909. (AC.)

Exposition also hosted college and other amateur baseball teams. The 1908 Pitt team poses on the Exposition Park bleachers. The cheap seats were just that—no frills and cheap to build. They were also open to the weather and susceptible to fire. (UP.)

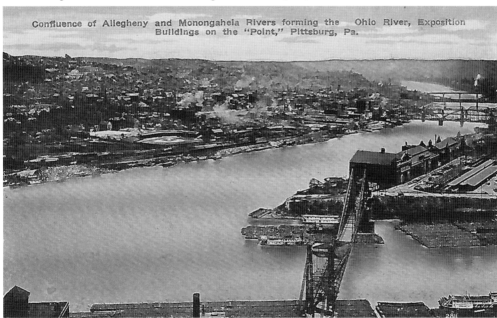

This period postcard places the ballpark in the context of the burgeoning cities of Allegheny and Pittsburgh. The wooden Union Bridge is gone, dating this to 1908 or after. The Point is at right. (AC.)

The Civil War Soldiers Monument stood on Monument Hill overlooking the ballpark and was often seen in photographs and postcards of Exposition Park. It also provided a vantage point for fans and photographers. Like today's Point Fountain, this was the most prominent and well-known feature of Pittsburgh. The shaft and the sculpture of "Fame" still stand in the Allegheny Commons a few blocks away, near the 1857 ballgame site. (LOC.)

Fans crowd Monument Hill to watch the Pirates' final game at Exposition on June 29, 1909. Only 5,545 paid their way into the park. The left field line bleachers and the rooftop boxes appear largely empty. The Pirates defeated the Cubs 8-1 at Old Exposition, but lost their opener at Forbes Field the next day with a crowd of 30,338, falling 3-2 to the Cubs. (AC.)

# LAST GASPS

## EXPOSITION PARK, 1910–1920

Though many of the grandstand seats were relocated to Forbes Field, there was life for the old park after the Pirates left. Sandlot, high school, and college teams used the field for baseball and football. Like Union Park and Recreation Park, proximity to the rail lines made it attractive for circuses and Wild West shows. Outdoor boxing matches were common, and a New Year's Day match was the biggest soccer event in the region. The park even hosted a parade of electrified Mardi Gras floats shipped up from New Orleans. A Thanksgiving Day football game became a big tradition for the local African American community, with future Negro baseball team owners Cum Posey and Sell Hall starring as players.

But without a regular tenant, the park suffered. Successive fires destroyed the training building and the clubhouse, though the grandstand was saved. A third fire took the center field fence. A local couple was arrested scavenging brass, iron, and rubber from the grandstand. Dreyfuss, who still held the lease, sold box seat chairs to a minor-league park in Steubenville, Ohio, and then had the grandstand dismantled. Salvaged lumber and brick were advertised for sale. The flagpole that held the championship pennants of 1901, 1902, and 1903 was moved to a local school. The field and bleachers remained. Exposition continued to host local baseball and football teams, and it also became a rumor magnet anytime a new baseball league was in the works to challenge the majors.

The year 1912 brought new life with the start of the United States League. Dreyfuss had allowed his lease to expire, and new rivals swooped in. The new club signed former Pirates star Deacon Phillippe as manager, and the team was quickly dubbed "the Filipinos," perhaps the oddest nickname in major-league history. The grandstand was rebuilt, "restored to its former likeness," according to the *Pittsburgh Press*, and opened on May 8 to a parade and an extra-inning loss.

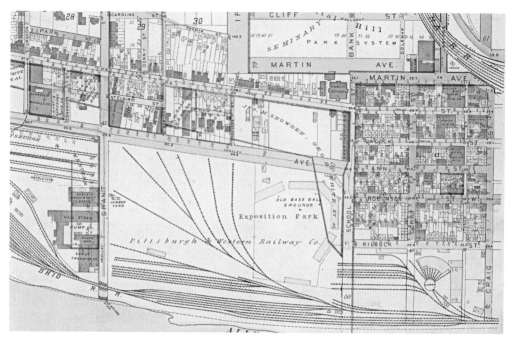

This 1910 insurance map shows the footprint of the "Old Baseball Grounds" as it stood after the departure of the Pirates in 1909. The map documents the location of the structures, including the grandstand, stair towers, bleachers, main entrance, and clubhouse. (UP.)

Baseball was very profitable by 1910, and those who could not buy into the National or American Leagues decided to create a rival league to compete for the baseball fans' allegiance and money. This photograph of the United States League owners includes Marshall Henderson, far left, co-owner of the Pittsburgh franchise and league vice president. The league president and driving force, Charles Witman of Reading, is fourth from left. (LOC.)

Deacon Phillippe (FILL-uh-pee), Pittsburgh's 1903 World Series hero in a losing cause, was hired as manager. On May 8, 1912, before 5,000 fans, his new team lost an 11-inning Opening Day heartbreaker, 3-2, to the Cincinnati Pippins. The Filipinos roared off to lead the new league, but by mid-June the United States League collapsed. Once again, fate had robbed the Deacon of a title. (LOC.)

In 1913, the Federal League took up the challenge to the major leagues, but flooding struck on March 29, inundating the park. Phillippe returned as manager, but the magic was gone. Renamed the Stogies, the team stumbled to a last-place finish, though Exposition was described as "the best ball field in the circuit." The 1913 version seen here lacked rooftop boxes, and the right field bleachers were open air. (UP.)

Changes came in 1914 with new ownership. Phillippe was not invited back, and the team was renamed the "Rebels" in a fan contest. The grandstand was largely rebuilt, rooftop boxes were added, and the right field bleachers gained a roof. A new clubhouse and entrance were built. This view from Monument Hill shows the main entrance and rooftop boxes, as well as Phipps Playground, a sandlot ball field across the street. (LOC.)

PITTSBURGH FROM MONUMENT HILL, NORTH SIDE, BY NIGHT, PITTSBURGH, PA.

This period postcard with a dramatic night view of the city is a fake! This is a copy of the previous image with a moon and tinting added to simulate night. This artist's night view of the city from Monument Hill provides a sense of how Exposition fit into its neighborhood on the "North Shore." (AC.)

This 1914 view from center field shows the new rooftop boxes. The edge of the new roof over the right field bleachers is just visible at left. High above the stadium stands the Civil War Soldiers Monument. (PP.)

Seen from downtown in 1915, the park is in its final configuration. Though Forbes Field and Philadelphia's Shibe Park had made wooden parks obsolete, Exposition Park still soldiered on. Note the figure-eight roller coaster at bottom left next to the Downtown Exposition Building. (UP.)

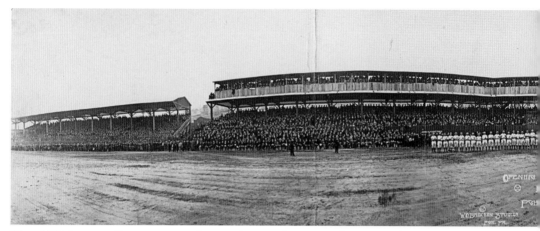

This 1915 Opening Day panorama distorts the stands into one horizontal line, but the features of the renovated park are clearly visible. While the left field line bleachers remain open air, the right field bleachers sport a roof. The rooftop boxes, eliminated in the 1913 version, returned in 1914. Hopes were high for 1915, and Opening Day drew 18,000 fans. The street parade included

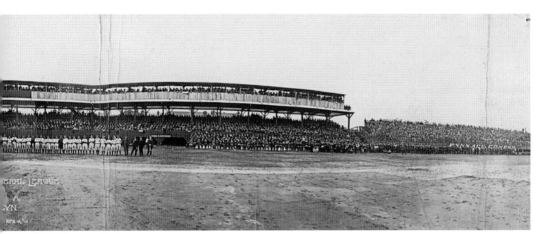

more than 100 cars containing players, politicians, league dignitaries, and prominent rooters. The Rebels led much of the 1915 season but faded in the final weekend, losing the pennant by a half game. (AC.)

Following the 1915 season, the Federal League owners made peace with the National and American Leagues and folded. This 1916 view shows the park still standing, but its days were numbered. Although sporting events continued on the field into the 1920s, the date of the demolition of the structures is unknown. Weeghman Park in Chicago is the only Federal League park that survives, better known today as Wrigley Field. (UP.)

## Murder Mystery Scenes
## Police on Blood Trail

Exposition reverted to hosting amateur, college, and semiprofessional teams, along with circuses and Wild West shows, but the stadium was also home to tramps, petty thieves, and worse. In September 1916, an unidentified man was found murdered under the left field bleachers. A local man confessed, recanted, was tried, and acquitted. One of the last photographs of Exposition is this newspaper shot of city detectives examining the bleachers. (*Pittsburgh Post.*)

# DREYFUSS'S FOLLY
## FORBES FIELD, 1909–1924

Fed up with lost revenue from canceled games and the costs of clean-up and repairs following floods, Dreyfuss began searching for a location for a new park that would stay high and dry. The last straw may have been the 1907 flood that not only inundated the park but also destroyed the covered wooden Union Bridge that connected Pittsburgh to Allegheny and connected the Pirates to their fans south of the river.

Real estate developer Franklin Nicola developed the Hotel Schenley (now Pitt Student Union) in Oakland in 1898 and, inspired by the "City Beautiful" movement, was aggressively pursuing development of this largely rural neighborhood three miles from Downtown Pittsburgh. Andrew Carnegie became a partner and built his flagship Carnegie Institute in Oakland. Carnegie helped Dreyfuss identify seven acres near the institute, far from any rivers.

Some mocked Dreyfuss for moving his team so far from the population centers and his existing fan base in Allegheny. But the big open spaces meant that the design of the park was not as constrained by existing city streets as other parks were, and Dreyfuss was free to build expansively.

No one had yet designed a concrete-and-steel ballpark, so Dreyfuss had to seek out an architect with parallel experience. As a horse-racing fan, Dreyfuss was familiar with the work of Charles W. Leavitt Jr., designer of the grandstands at Belmont Park and Saratoga Racetrack. Forbes Field was to be Leavitt's only ballpark.

Although Forbes Field opened to universal acclaim in 1909, Dreyfuss continually tinkered with the park. He acquired additional land and expanded the already spacious outfield. The orientation of the playing field and the location of the left field foul pole changed in both 1911 and 1912. Scoreboards were replaced as new technology became available. Entrances, turnstiles, and ticket windows would change in an effort to improve fan access. Strong demand for tickets motivated expansion of seating on several occasions. Forbes Field was not frozen. It was continually evolving.

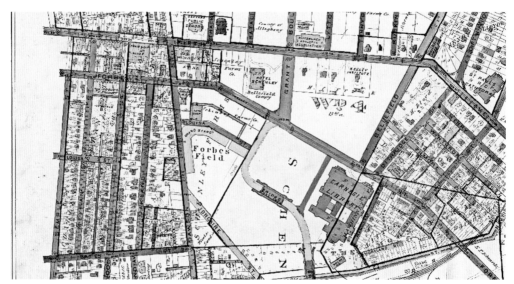

This 1910 Hopkins Insurance map places Forbes Field in the largely undeveloped Oakland neighborhood. The two major arteries, Forbes and Fifth Avenues, show few structures along their routes. The Hotel Schenley, Carnegie Library, and the St. Pierre Ravine Bridge are identified. (UP.)

This series of five photographs shows the late stages of Forbes Field's construction. Grading of the site began in January 1909, and construction started March 1. Just four months later, the first game was played on June 30. As seen here, curious fans could enter the construction site to view the work. (PAM.)

The contractor, naturally, was Nicola Building Company. This June 9 image shows the seats being installed. Forbes would seat 23,000 in its original configuration, nearly 10,000 more than Exposition and the largest capacity in the major leagues. (PAM.)

By June 15, the infield has taken shape, and workmen are filling in the foul ground. The distance between home plate and the stands was 110 feet, making for huge foul ground. Note the railcar and tracks to enable the men to efficiently bring in gravel, soils, and sod. The bleachers in right center are distant but appear to be largely complete. (PAM.)

Just 10 days from opening and a crew is spreading out the tarp. Pirates manager Fred Clarke had invented a mechanical system for deploying a tarp, and it debuted at Exposition Park in 1906. He received a patent in 1911. Clarke was very involved in the design of Forbes Field and was regularly consulted on its details. (PAM.)

Here is the view from Forbes Field toward Schenley Park. The unfinished left field bleachers are just visible at bottom left. St. Pierre's Ravine, center, would be filled in in 1915. The bridge is still there—it was just buried! (PAM.)

This artist's rendering appeared on the cover of the inaugural game program and was a popular image on postcards. This is what Dreyfuss had been dreaming of and planning for. This view provides a good sense of the large scale of Forbes Field and its place in the Oakland landscape. (AC.)

Here is a full view of the grandstand from Schenley Park at the inaugural game on June 30, 1909. The flag flies at half-staff because the National League had seen the death of two owners in 10 days—John Dovey of the Boston Doves and Israel Durham of the Philadelphia Phillies. St. Pierre's Ravine Bridge is at right. (LOC.)

Perhaps because of the bunting, this view has often been mistakenly attributed to the 1909 World Series, but it is the unfinished exterior during the inaugural week in 1909. Tarps and wood slats cover the locations of the third-level windows. The awning frame over the main entrance has been installed but not the awning roof—the flags are hanging right through the frame. (LOC.)

Compare this with the previous image. All work is now complete. The tarps and wood cladding are gone, and the top windows have been installed. The awning is complete. Offices filled the second floor with a private apartment above, but after the 1909 World Series, Dreyfuss mused about creating a trophy room in place of the apartment. (LOC.)

As fans entered through the arches of the grandstand, they funneled into lanes for the turnstiles. This is the original configuration from 1909, which was included in a book by the architect. Dreyfuss would tinker with the turnstile locations, ticket windows, entrances for season ticket holders and the press, and other details of his new park. Forbes Field was not static. (PF.)

Not everything changed with the new park. Fans still exited across the field after games. This real-photo postcard shows the crowd departing after a game. The right-center bleachers are at top right, and the original hand-operated scoreboard is at center below the flag pole. (AC.)

This sequence of five photographs provides a 360-degree view of Forbes as originally built. This view of the grandstands begins near the end of the right field stands and stretches around past home. The first base dugout and the screen behind home are clearly visible. (LOC.)

The sequence continues with the third base side. The rain tarp is visible in front of the stands at center. Note the rooftop seating, reminiscent of Exposition Park, and the gate separating the grandstand from the left field bleachers. (LOC.)

The left field bleachers remained open air throughout the park's life. Note the foul pole in its original location in front of the bleachers. In 1912, the field was reconfigured to move the foul pole to the left field corner. Like Exposition Park, the field slopes up to the wall, and some in the overflow crowd are taking advantage for a better view. The top of the original scoreboard is at bottom right. (LOC.)

The right center bleachers are packed. They would be a feature of the park until removed in the 1925 expansion. Beyond are the fairly fashionable houses of the Oakland neighborhood. Just like the earlier view of Exposition Park's bleachers, this crowd is almost entirely men and boys. At the far end of the front row, a police officer keeps an eye on the crowd. (LOC.)

Completing the 360-degree tour, the end of the right field grandstand served as utilitarian space for the grounds crew. Laundry is hanging in front of unused temporary bleachers. Tarps and tools are scattered about. For large crowds, this area accommodated temporary bleachers and standing room. Outside the park are houses on Boquet Street. In 1911, several boys were arrested for climbing on the roofs to watch a ballgame. (LOC.)

This view of the new ballpark from beyond center field shows the rear of the right field bleachers, the flagpole, and the steep slope that would challenge the builders in the 1925 expansion. As built in 1909, Forbes Field could seat 23,000, the largest capacity in baseball. Successful teams drove demand for tickets, so Dreyfuss regularly tinkered to add capacity. (UP.)

The 1909 World Series was the hot ticket in Pittsburgh, and if a fan could not get one, he had to get creative! These men climbed a utility pole beyond the left field wall to get a glimpse of the local heroes fighting for the championship. (LOC.)

Here is another pair of pole-sitters! Joncaire Street sloped sharply downhill beyond the right field corner, which would present difficulties when the park was expanded in 1925 with the creation of the right field pavilion. This view shows the back of the right field wall and the right-center bleachers. In 1920, a 29-year-old man was seriously injured when he fell down this slope, apparently looking for free entry to the park. (UP.)

Game No. 1 against the American League champion Detroit Tigers in 1909 was the first World Series game at Forbes Field. Barney Dreyfuss (first row, second from left) and his entourage are seen here in the box seats. They are a serious-looking group but finished the day happy when the Bucs won 4-1 behind Babe Adams's pitching and a home run by player-manager Fred Clarke. (CMOA.)

When Forbes opened, Louisa Street was a "paper street," owned by the city but never built. By 1910, it was revealed that Dreyfuss had built the stadium over the city's right-of-way. Technically, the city could demand that the grandstand be demolished, but that was politically impossible. Dreyfuss simply relocated and finished the street along the third base line, then donated it to the city. (AC.)

By 1911, Dreyfuss sought to lease a half acre of Schenley Park to expand left field. The city was willing, but Mary Schenley's deed of gift limited the use to parks, art, and science. Baseball did not seem to fit the criteria; thus, this cartoon lampooning the team's argument. But baseball was popular, and Dreyfuss got his sliver. A new wall was built for 1911, eliminating the sloped terrace. (*Pittsburgh Gazette-Times.*)

This period postcard shows the original left field wall and the coveted portion of Schenley Park. The land sloped away from the rear of the wall, requiring a considerable amount of fill. The original field was turtle-backed, with a low swale behind the infield to aid drainage. In 1911, a new drainage system was added and the outfield leveled. While the fill settled, left field was not resodded until 1912. (AC.)

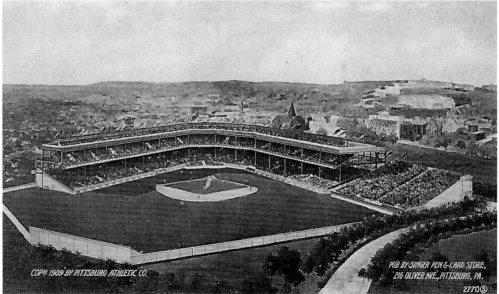

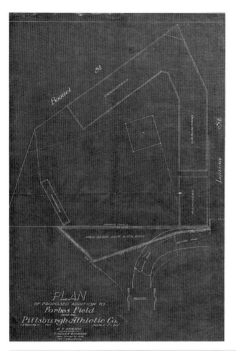

This blueprint shows how the park expanded in left field, including rerouting a portion of a city street. News accounts of the time suggest that the diamond was adjusted to move the right field line slightly away from the end of the stands, but the left field foul pole still intersected the front of the bleachers. The work was completed in May while the team was on a road trip. (PF.)

The original scoreboard was located in center field next to the flagpole and the outfield bleachers. It was hand-operated, much like the Exposition Park scoreboard. It can be seen here in a grainy newspaper photograph during the raising of the 1909 World Championship banner. Being more than 450 feet from home, it must have been difficult to see. (*Pittsburgh Post.*)

## RAISING THE WORLD'S FLAG

Crowd in right-field bleachers has an inning when Fred Clarke starts pulling the cord and the great banner is drawn to the top of the tall staff at Forbes field.

New for 1911 was an electric scoreboard, located near the site of the original beside the right field bleachers. The new board was twice as big and was controlled from the press box. It was state of the art, providing info on games around the league. Here, it is seen during the Pitt–Penn State game in 1911. The flagpole now obscured the scoreboard and would be moved against the outfield wall in 1912. (UP.)

Unlike scoreboards elsewhere, the one at Forbes Field had no advertising, at Dreyfuss's insistence. The outfield walls and scoreboard would remain ad-free until well after his death. In other ballparks of the time, like Brooklyn's Ebbets Field, advertising abounded. Here, the University of Pittsburgh band poses in front of the scoreboard in 1912 or 1913. The band was organized in 1911 and first obtained uniforms in 1912. (UP.)

As originally configured, the left field line ended in front of the bleachers, creating a short distance of 305 feet to the foul pole, topped here by a US flag. This also created confusion on fair or foul balls, and conflict between players and rabid fans. In 1912, the foul lines were moved so the foul pole was at the far end of the bleachers, 360 feet from home. (LOC.)

This 1912 game against Brooklyn shows the relocated left field foul pole in the left field corner where it would remain. The sloped terrace at the left field wall is gone. Other 1912 improvements included added box seats, expanded dugouts, and an entrance under the grandstand for umpires and visiting players. The playing field would retain this basic configuration until 1925. (PP.)

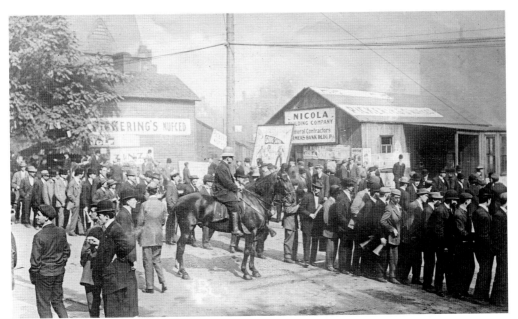

Average fans had to queue up for tickets. In this scene outside the ballpark in 1912, more than 30 men wait in line while a mounted policeman keeps watch. Several men hold megaphones. In the background is a shed of the Nicola Building Company, the contractors who built Forbes and constructed the various alterations in its early years. (LOC.)

This demure street scene near the ballpark was captured at the memorial to political boss Christopher Magee, whose Oakland home became Magee Women's Hospital. Magee's nephew William would become mayor and helped Dreyfuss hoist the 1909 World Championship pennant. The left field bleachers are visible at left, and the Schenley Hotel is at right. This monument remains in its original location. (AC.)

This panorama shows a 1915 football game between the University of Pittsburgh and archrival Washington & Jefferson College. Pitt won this battle of unbeatens 19-0 en route to a perfect 8-0 season under coach "Pop" Warner. Temporary bleachers are seen against the left field wall and the end of the right field grandstand. Pitt would play its home games at Forbes Field until

In 1917, Pitt again went undefeated at 10-0, outscoring opponents 260-31. Their biggest game was against Washington & Jefferson at Forbes Field. Here, Washington & Jefferson's John Tressel makes a leaping catch, but Pitt eked out a 13-0 victory. Pitt's Jock Sutherland was a consensus All-American in 1917 and would become Pitt's coach in 1924. Bunting and flags demonstrate patriotic fervor with US entry into World War I earlier that year. (UP.)

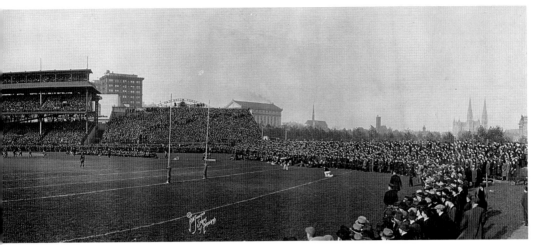

the opening of Pitt Stadium in 1925. Forbes Field would also host Duquesne University's football team, a national powerhouse in the 1930s. On November 1, 1929, Forbes Field was the site of the first night game in college football as Duquesne defeated Thiel College. (LOC.)

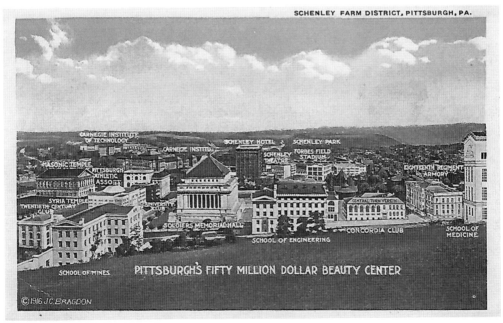

By 1916, Oakland's building boom was filling the landscape. This vintage postcard labeled the prominent buildings in Pittsburgh's "Beauty Center," including Forbes Field. At center is the Schenley Hotel, built in 1898, the first piece in Franklin Nicola's vision. It became popular with visiting ball clubs. At lower right is the Concordia Club where Dreyfuss was a prominent member. No one mentioned "folly." Dreyfuss had chosen wisely. (AC.)

In 1922, an enormous lighted sign and clock for the *Pittsburgh Post* newspaper was erected outside the park and dominated the view beyond right field, day and night. When the right field pavilion was added, the sign was raised, but the *Pittsburgh Post* merged into the *Pittsburgh Gazette* in 1927, and the sign was soon abandoned. (*Pittsburgh Post.*)

The paper anthropomorphized the clock, running a column of game notes under the heading "What Post Clock Saw." The paper awarded $100 to any player hitting a home run in the vicinity of the clock. Reb Russell, a star pitcher until his arm gave out, remade himself as a slugging outfielder and cashed three checks from the *Pittsburgh Post* in his two years with the Pirates. (*Pittsburgh Post.*)

# GROWTH

## FORBES FIELD, 1925–1937

The years following the 1909 World Series triumph found the Pirates among the top three teams in the National League but well off the pace for the pennant. By 1914, the team had slid to the second division, culminating in a 103-loss season in 1917. After that season, and a short stint as manager, Honus Wagner retired, later rejoining the team as a much-beloved coach. The Pirates manager in 1917 was Hugo Bezdek, who would find greater fame as coach of Penn State's football team, winning the Rose Bowl in 1923. In 1937, he became the first coach of the Cleveland Rams football team, making him the only man to lead both a Major League Baseball and a National Football League team.

Dreyfuss began to assemble a strong team in the early 1920s. Future hall of famers Max Carey, Kiki Cuyler, and Pie Traynor formed the core of the team, complemented by a strong pitching staff. With fan interest and attendance growing, Dreyfuss decided to undertake the biggest expansion in Forbes Field's history. The relocation of the University of Pittsburgh football team to the new Pitt Stadium after the 1924 season finally gave Dreyfuss a construction season to make his big changes.

Dreyfuss's timing was once again perfect. Just as in 1909, his capital investment paid off when the Pirates won the World Series. The 1925 team roared back from a 3-1 deficit and defeated the Washington Senators. The Pirates returned to the World Series in 1927 with Paul and Lloyd Waner joining Pie Traynor and Kiki Cuyler, but they had the misfortune of facing the 1927 "Murderers' Row" Yankees and were swept in four games.

The team remained competitive through the 1930s, but the ballpark remained largely unchanged until 1938.

# Proposed Forbes Field Improvements

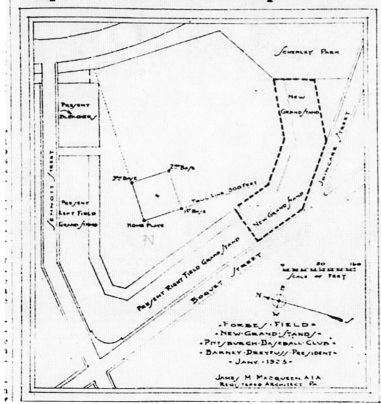

In 1924, Dreyfuss added 2,000 seats in three rows of field-level boxes, but more were needed. In 1925, he proposed a double-deck right field grandstand. This sketch by the architect shows the proposed expansion and dimensions as it was squeezed into the site, bounded by steeply sloped Joncaire Street beyond the right field corner. (PP.)

The view over the Schenley Fountain in 1925 shows the new right field pavilion and the back of the new scoreboard in left-center field. This scoreboard, the third in the park's history, would remain in this location only for the 1925 season. (PF.)

The 1925 team is posed against the grandstand behind home, providing an uncommon view of the seating area without fans. The exposed steel structure was part of the park's defining visual elements and part of its charm in a city that produced steel for the nation. (PP.)

Despite the expansion, ticket demand for the World Series was heavy. The team moved the new scoreboard to the left field corner and erected temporary bleachers over and in front of the left field and center field walls. Seats were even added in front of the scoreboard, foreshadowing the Greenberg Gardens/Kiner's Korner area more than two decades later. (PP.)

# FORBES FIELD

JUNE 30
1909 25th 1934

BARNEY DREYFUSS
1865 •• 1932
President, Pittsburgh Base Ball Club
1903 •• 1932

SAMUEL W. DREYFUSS
1896 •• 1931
Treasurer, Pittsburgh Base Ball Club
1920 •• 1931

# ANNIVERSARY

The team celebrated the park's 25th anniversary in 1934. Barney Dreyfuss had died two years earlier. He had intended that his son Sam succeed him as team president, but Sam died tragically in 1931. Dreyfuss's son-in-law Bill Benswanger would head the team until 1946. This view shows temporary bleachers built for the 1925 World Series. (PP.)

The Dreyfuss Monument was dedicated during the 25th anniversary event with National League president John Heydler placing a wreath. Originally located in play in deep center field, it was later relocated to Three Rivers Stadium. It can be found today on the concourse behind home plate at PNC Park. Also unveiled at that 1934 game was a new public address system, eliminating the megaphone used by the announcer. (*Pittsburgh Press.*)

On May 25, 1935, in his final season, Babe Ruth came to Forbes as a member of the Boston Braves. For one day, Ruth recaptured the glory, hitting three home runs, the last being the first to clear the roof of the right field pavilion. Here is Ruth heading home after that final clout. He would retire just a week later. Note the left field scoreboard. (PP.)

This vintage postcard shows the ballpark that Ruth would have seen in his last moment of glory. The right field pavilion is only 300 feet down the line, but it towers above the corner. The Crow's Nest (1938) and light towers (1940) are still a few years away. The densely packed neighborhood squeezes the ball field. (AC.)

This early aerial view of Schenley Plaza puts Forbes into the context of its Oakland neighborhood. The Mary Schenley Fountain is the focal point, with Schenley Park beyond and Carnegie Library at left. The trees are young and only hint at the forested backdrop that would become part of Forbes Field's image. Over time, the grassy oval at center would be paved for parking. (UP.)

This aerial view shows Forbes Field at lower left and Pitt Stadium, built in 1925, at center. The top floors of the Cathedral of Learning are unfinished, dating this photograph to about 1930. Downtown is at top with the future site of Three Rivers Stadium across the river at top center. (UP.)

It was a different time! To avoid a rainout of a large and profitable Fourth of July crowd in 1936, the grounds crew resorted to pouring gasoline on the soaked field and burning it off to dry it enough to be playable. This was not a unique event. Other photographs show similar efforts at other times. (*Pittsburgh Sun-Telegraph.*)

AFTER THE RAIN . . . GASOLINE MAKES IT POSSIBLE FOR GAME TO CONTINUE

This 1935 exterior view of the home plate entrance at the corner of Sennott and Boquet Streets shows an unadorned utilitarian streetscape with a row of homes across from the 1B grandstand. The press gate and the season ticketholders' entrance are a short distance down Boquet Street (also sometimes written as "Bouqet Street"). These were created in 1924 when more turnstiles and ticket windows were added. (UP.)

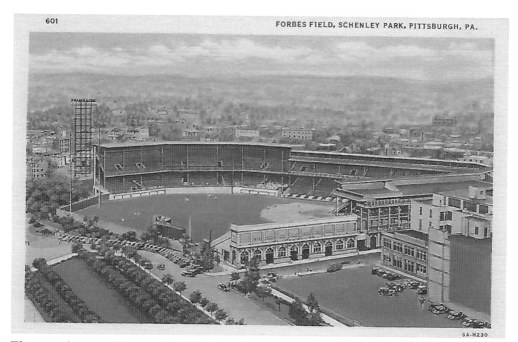

This period postcard shows the new pavilion as it looms over right field. Gone are the bleachers in right-center. The abandoned frame of the old *Pittsburgh Post* sign still stands at left. The limits of the site created a short 300-foot distance to the right field foul pole. In 1932, a 14.5-foot screen was added to the pavilion to eliminate cheap home runs. (AC.)

Although this photograph dates to 1960, it provides an excellent idea of the view that fans had from the new right field pavilion. The right fielder is not visible in this image. With the short distance from home, he would be playing fairly close to the wall and not fully visible to fans seated in the pavilion. Football markings are visible. (PP.)

# LOST HERITAGE
## NEGRO LEAGUE PARKS

In 1884, two brothers joined the Toledo Blue Stockings of the American Association. Moses Fleetwood "Fleet" Walker was an excellent defensive catcher, and when injuries hit Toledo, his younger brother Weldy joined the club for five games. They were the first and last African Americans to play Major League Baseball until 1947, when Jackie Robinson joined the Dodgers.

Fleet made at least one trip to play the Alleghenies at Recreation Park, making him the first black to play major-league ball in Pittsburgh, and he was greeted graciously by the local press. His brother Weldy would wait a bit longer to appear in Pittsburgh.

By 1885, blacks were barred from major-league clubs, though several dozen played in various minor leagues before the opportunity closed in those leagues as well.

The Pittsburgh Keystones were formed in 1887 to play in the new League of Colored Baseball Players. The team considered Exposition I as its home ground, but ultimately chose Recreation Park. The team opened at home on May 6, losing to the Gorhams of New York 11-8. The team included Weldy Walker and a young King Solomon "Sol" White, who would go on to be a star player, manager, and the first historian of African American baseball. He was inducted into Cooperstown in 2006. The Keystones got off to a 3-4 start, but the league folded in slightly more than a week. The Keystones would continue playing at Recreation as an independent team, with Weldy managing the team in 1888.

For the next 30 years, black baseball in Pittsburgh consisted of independent professional and semiprofessional teams, some of which built strong reputations. In 1920, Rube Foster founded the Negro National League with the goal of creating a stable professional league with black ownership. In Pittsburgh, a Barbadian immigrant and businessman, Alexander McDonald Williams, wanted to be part of Foster's new league.

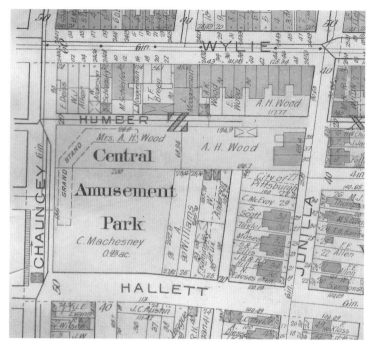

Alexander McDonald Williams became a successful pool hall owner in Pittsburgh's Hill District, but his doctor advised him to get into a business with some fresh air. Williams chose "the baseball," as his wife referred to this new venture. In 1920, he built a wooden park on a vacant lot in the Hill District, shown here on an insurance map. (UP.)

In 1920, Williams hired a young African American architect, Louis Bellinger, to design a ballpark, and they hired local African American contractors to build the wooden park. Williams called it Central Amusement Park, soon simplified as Central Park. This is the only known photograph of the park. (UP.)

In 1921, Williams formed the Pittsburgh Keystones and joined the Negro National League (NNL) as an associate member. The Keystones could play league teams, but games would not be counted in the league's standings. Late in 1921, Foster and his American Giants made a ballyhooed trip to play the Keystones at Central Park. In this photograph of NNL owners, Williams is in the third row, third from right, and Rube Foster is in the first row, third from left. (WFA.)

In 1922, the Keystones became a full member, but finished sixth in an eight team league. It was a financial disaster. Williams folded the Keystones and gave up his league membership. The dream had died. Central Park remained for a few more seasons, hosting independent black teams, including a new version of the Keystones, shown here. By July 1925, the Homestead Grays squeezed out other local black teams, and Central Park was dismantled. (Pittsburgh Courier.)

This 1930s aerial view shows three Negro League parks within a few blocks in Pittsburgh's Hill District. The white scar at lower left is the demolished Central Park, still a vacant lot today. Ammon Field is at top center, and Greenlee Field is at right. (CMUAA.)

This desolate image of Humber Way from 1934 may contain the last vestige of Central Park. At far left is a wooden footbridge that crosses over Chauncey Way, connecting pedestrians to the site of the ballpark at left. Given that nothing was built on this site before or after Central Park, the only reason for the footbridge was to provide access to the grandstand. The footbridge is also now gone. (UP.)

In the 1920s, Ammon Field was home to early versions of the Grays and Crawfords. As a municipal field, the city would not permit teams to charge admission. Clearly, a better home field was needed. Ammon was demolished in 1939, and the city built a new field one block west, now named Josh Gibson Field. No photographs of Ammon's grandstand have surfaced, but this 1938 newspaper sketch shows its location and orientation. (Pittsburgh Courier.)

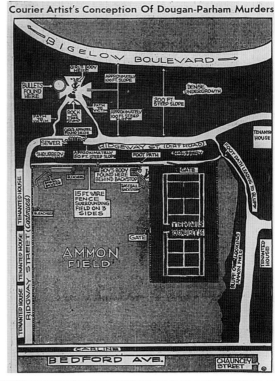

Greenlee Field was the solution to the ballpark problem. In 1931, the Depression hit the Entress Brick Works hard, so the white owners were receptive when approached by a local black numbers boss. Gus Greenlee became the primary backer of the Crawfords, a local sandlot team, that he would transform into national champions. This aerial view shows the park hard against Bedford Avenue. The architect was Louis Bellinger, designer of Central Park 12 years earlier. (CMUAA.)

This aerial view was taken from beyond left field. Bedford Avenue is at top. Lincoln Cemetery borders the park at right, and the municipal hospital is beyond right field at far left. The hand-operated scoreboard is in left field. The park opened April 29, 1932, to much fanfare. Although Greenlee's name was on the ballpark and he was the public face of the operation, he was only a minority owner—a 25-percent share to his white partners' 75 percent. (CMUAA.)

This sequence of four photographs shows the Bedford Avenue exterior, moving uphill from west to east. The west end of the structure housed offices and clubhouses. Because of the slope of Bedford Avenue, the grandstand was built atop the two-story brick structure. The picket fence encloses the cemetery, and its entrance gate is behind the telephone pole, right up against the ballpark. The arched entrance gates to the field are at far right. (CMUAA.)

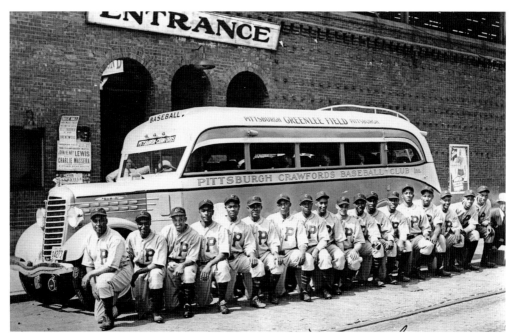

The 1936 Crawfords pose in front of their team bus on Bedford Avenue in front of Greenlee Field. The three arched openings in the brick facade are the main entrance to the grandstand. Fans walked up steps to field level. The caption reads, "Champions Negro National League 1935," but the poster advertises a boxing match between Greenlee protégé John Henry Lewis against Charlie Massera on May 27, 1936. (PP.)

Continuing uphill on Bedford Avenue are the gates to the bleachers along the right field line. Greenlee Field was also used for boxing matches, midget car races, community festivals, and amateur football games. The Pittsburgh Pirates football team, later renamed the Steelers, held in-season practices here during the 1930s. (CMUAA.)

At the eastern edge of the park is the vehicle gate. The slope of Bedford Avenue has risen to finally meet the field level. The men in the photograph were part of the architectural team that was designing the public housing complex that would replace the field. They took the time to document the park before its demolition after the 1938 season. (CMUAA.)

The Homestead Grays also used Greenlee Field as their home park when Forbes Field was unavailable. The 1937 team is posed in short right field with a view of the right field bleachers and the fence separating the park from the municipal hospital. Josh Gibson is third from right in the second row. (PP.)

This view from deep in center field to the empty grandstand shows a spacious park. A grandstand roof was planned but never built, leaving fans complaining about rain and summer heat and hurting attendance. The lights were added in 1932 and inaugurated with a game between the Crawfords and Grays on September 16, 1932. Forbes Field would not add lights until 1940. (CMUAA.)

The grandstand behind home is packed for a day game. Baseball was popular and an important part of the culture of the prosperous black community in the Hill District. It was viewed as safe and welcoming for women and families, both evident in this photograph. Note the young beer vendor with a bucket at right. Greenlee's partners would not allow him to hire black employees, creating resentment in the community. (CMOA.)

One of the last events held at Greenlee Field was an exhibition softball game on September 9, 1938, by a barnstorming team led by boxing champion Joe Louis, seen here holding a young relative. Greenlee was losing money on his baseball venture and folded the Crawfords after the 1938 season. The city was looking to build public housing, and Greenlee and his partners agreed to sell. The field was demolished within months. (CMOA.)

Following the demolition of Greenlee Field, the Homestead Grays conducted practices, exhibition games, and occasional Negro National League games at West Field in Munhall, Pennsylvania, up the hill from Homestead. Built in 1937 by the borough, the field survived largely intact until replaced on the same site in 2017. The Borough Building beyond right field still stands. (ROS.)

LOST HERITAGE: NEGRO LEAGUE PARKS

David B. Stinson of deadballbaseball.com photographed the dilapidated but largely intact park in 2015, and provided this sequence of four images. This view of the exterior of the grandstand shows the basic structure and the neglect it suffered. Because the streets did not extend to the grandstand, teams and most fans arrived from the outfield. In later years, the concourse behind home became a dumping ground. (DB.)

The seating bowl was better maintained, hosting high school and amateur games for many years. Like Greenlee Field, the park never had a roof. A walkway behind the top of the stands extended the length of the seating area and provided easy circulation. (DB.)

The Grays played Negro National League games here when Forbes Field was unavailable. The Negro National League folded after the 1948 season, and the Grays struggled along as an independent team until 1951. From the third base side, the long run of stands along the right field line made the park ideal for football games as well as baseball. (DB.)

The dugouts were occupied by all the greats of the local and visiting Negro League teams, including Pittsburgh's own Josh Gibson. Although it was one of the last tangible links to the Negro League era, the borough demolished the structure and replaced it with a new ballpark in 2017. The field remains, but little else. (DB.)

# HOUSE OF THRILLS
## FORBES FIELD, 1938–1970

With a second-place finish in 1937, the Pirates felt confident about a 1938 pennant. The team boasted five future hall of famers: Arky Vaughan and Paul and Lloyd Waner led the offense, Pie Traynor managed, and Honus Wagner coached. Anticipating postseason crowds and heavy media coverage, the team added the Crow's Nest, a roofed seating section on top of the existing grandstand roof behind home, and an expanded press box with an elevator. Sadly, team president Bill Benswanger did not have the same luck as father-in-law Barney Dreyfuss in 1909 and 1925. The team faded down the stretch and finished two games behind the Chicago Cubs.

The war years were not kind to the Pirates, and the 1950s were worse. They would lose more than 100 games in three straight seasons, and aside from the slugging exploits of Ralph Kiner, fans had little reason to hope or cheer. Things began to brighten with the debuts of Roberto Clemente in 1955 and Bill Mazeroski in 1956.

The 1960 team is still adored in Pittsburgh memory. The team's penchant for late-inning comeback victories gave Forbes a new nickname—the House of Thrills. The greatest thrill came on October 13, 1960, when Mazeroski's home run in Game No. 7 of the World Series defeated the New York Yankees and entered the realm of legend. Fans still gather at the remnants of the left field wall each October to listen to the broadcast and to relive the emotions of that game.

Forbes Field was a complex structure, and much of its charm and lore lie in the park's details, its lively urban location, and the ways that fans engaged with the park and the game. This chapter illustrates some of those details and the fan experience that made the park's demolition a melancholy episode still regretted by many a half century later.

The ballpark's fate was sealed in 1958 when it was purchased by the University of Pittsburgh, but it was leased back to the team until a new park could be built.

Here is an exterior close-up of the Crow's Nest, added in 1938 in anticipation of a pennant run that fizzled. An elevator serviced the rooftop seating and expanded press box. The Crow's Nest became a defining element of the ballpark, instantly recognizable in photographs from 1938 until the stadium's closing in 1970. (PP.)

The Crow's Nest is prominent in this view of an empty ballpark. The original press box and broadcast booth are seen slung beneath the second tier, and a new broadcast booth is on the left side of the Crow's Nest. (PP.)

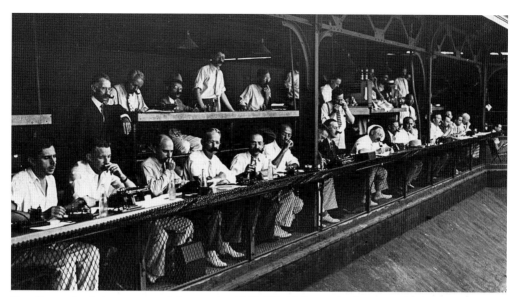

Dreyfuss valued the press, and during the 1909 World Series, he became the first to provide a free buffet for the writers. Here is the press box in 1939. The fake handlebar mustaches were part of a celebration of baseball's centennial, when Abner Doubleday supposedly invented the game, a story now known to be apocryphal. (PP.)

Here is a view into the park over the left field bleachers during the first night game at Forbes, June 4, 1940. Greenlee Field had permanent lights in 1932, and Negro League teams occasionally used temporary lights at Forbes Field, but the Pirates waited until the eve of World War II to install permanent lights. The packed parking lot is evidence that the move was popular with fans. (PP.)

While other owners reaped easy cash from lucrative billboard ads, the Dreyfuss family continued Barney's ban on advertising, with one exception. In 1943, a large plywood US Marine towered above the left-center wall with a sign promoting war bonds. He was in play and capable of robbing a slugger of a home run. This photograph shows an amateur game on the field. The Marine only lasted one season. (UP.)

From that same amateur game in 1943, the dugout and box seats are seen in a rare close-up. The spartan dugout is backed by horizontal beadboard. The box seats extend only to the back wall of the dugout, and they have folding chairs rather than stadium seats. (UP.)

In 1947, the Pirates acquired the famed Detroit Tiger slugger Hank Greenberg, who lost four years to military service during the war. To improve the pull hitter's prospects, the bullpens were moved from foul ground to a new fenced-in section in front of the scoreboard and left field wall. This shortened the home run distance by 30 feet. Here, post holes have been dug for the fence on what would be dubbed "Greenberg Gardens." (PP.)

The new fence is complete in front of the scoreboard, which is topped by the round Gruen clock. This was later replaced by a square Longines clock. Greenberg hit 25 home runs in 1947 and then retired to take a front-office job with the Cleveland Indians, but the Pirates discovered a new power hitter that year, and the fenced area became "Kiner's Korner." (PP.)

This aerial photograph shows Greenberg Gardens in left field. The batting cage can be seen stored on the field against the center field wall next to the flagpole. Before 1942, it was stored behind home in front of the stands. In 1942, a larger cage arrived and was stored in foul ground along the right field line, but it was moved to center field in 1943 where it remained. (PAM.)

Another aerial view shows how the stadium was adapted for football. The Steelers would use Forbes as their home field from 1933 until 1963. In 1958, the team began playing some games at larger Pitt Stadium and left Forbes completely after the 1963 season. (PAM.)

House of Thrills: Forbes Field, 1938–1970

The 1955 Steelers pose in front of the scoreboard. Beside the round Gruen clock is a square Western Union clock that counted down the 15-minute quarters. It was put up only for football season. The 1955 team started 4-1 but lost seven straight to finish last in the NFL. (AC.)

This interior view of the right field side shows the box seats stretching to the rear wall of the dugout. The box seats were expanded several times during the stadium's life by adding rows to the front, adding seats and ticket revenue without major changes to the structure. (PP.)

This undated night view shows the left field side with the final expansion of the box seats to a point parallel to the front of the dugouts. The scoreboard now boasts the square Longines clock, which replaced the round Gruen clock in 1958. (PP.)

This daytime aerial view shows the completed stadium in its final configuration. The box seats extend to the front edge of the dugout. The square Longines clock tops the scoreboard. But there are signs of the ballpark's age. The roof of the right field pavilion looks to consist of patches on patches on patches. (PP.)

The broadcast booth hung beneath the second deck. WWSW broadcast the games from 1938 to 1954 with Rosey Rowswell as the announcer, seen here in a hat, seated above the left edge of the sign. Next to him is Bing Crosby, who became a part owner of the Pirates in 1947. (CMOA.)

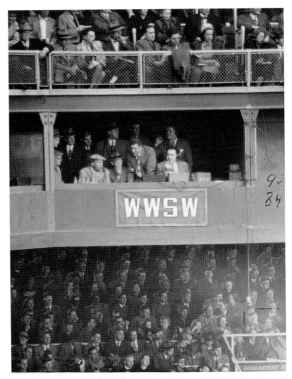

Rowswell created one of the most unique home run calls in broadcasting, calling on the fictional Aunt Minnie to "open the window!" when a Pirate batter hit a long drive. An assistant would drop a pan full of nuts and bolts, simulating the crash of breaking glass. "Too bad. Aunt Minnie didn't make it!" Here is Rowswell and his fictional Aunt Minnie on the field in front of the grandstand in a promo for KDKA television. (PP.)

When Rowswell died unexpectedly in February 1955, his assistant was ready to take the reins. Bob Prince began work as Rowswell's partner in 1947 and often had to drop the pan to simulate the demise of poor Aunt Minnie's window. Prince is seen here in a rare interior shot of the unadorned broadcast booth at Forbes. (PP.)

Another rare interior view shows Roberto Clemente at his locker in the Pirates clubhouse. The locker consists of bare unpainted plywood with a nameplate, a few hooks, and a spot to stack bats. The Rawlings jersey is marked "Clemente 61," perhaps indicating the year. (PP.)

Honus Wagner was a Pirates player and coach over more than 50 years. In April 1955, a statue was unveiled in Schenley Park, just beyond the left field wall. Here, Wagner is seated before the statue and various dignitaries at the dedication. Fellow hall of famer Cy Young attended the ceremony. Before the end of the year, both greats would pass on. The statue moved to Three Rivers in 1971 and now stands at PNC Park. (PP.)

Lights were added to the park in 1940. Here, local neighborhood old-timers relax in the park beyond the left field wall on a pleasant summer evening, enjoying a game and a crowd that they can hear but not see. (PP.)

Fans lined up at Forbes for tickets or to get a good seat in the bleachers. Glass block and brick have filled in some of the archways of the old park, but many of the decorative elements of the original design are evident. From the clothing styles, this may date from the late 1940s or early 1950s, the heyday of Ralph Kiner. (PP.)

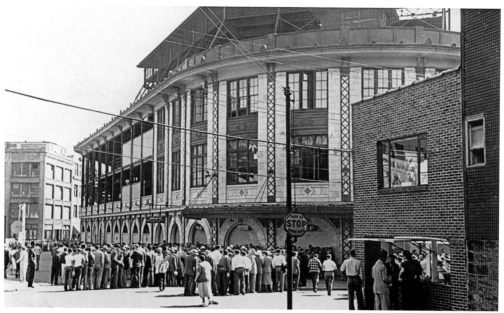

A crowd gathers to enter the grandstand while a few fans grab a pregame hot dog at the lunch counter across the street. The stadium created a bit of bustle on the streets even when attendance was modest. Fans rode the streetcars and buses on the main arteries a few blocks away or parked in the neighborhood. In either case, most walked through the neighborhood to and from the park. (PP.)

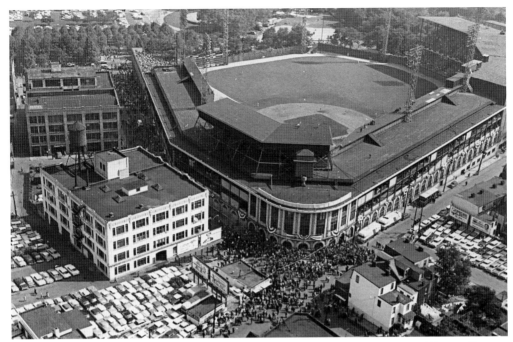

This aerial view shows the activity outside the home plate entrance at Sennott and Boquet Streets. The residential character of the area has begun to degrade. Sites that were desirable homes when Forbes was built in 1909 are now more valuable for parking and hot dog stands. But the urban locale ensured a lively street scene before and after games. (PP.)

Another aerial view puts Forbes Field in its neighborhood context. Pitt's Cathedral of Learning looms at right with the Stephen Foster Theater (1937) at its base. The round Gruen clock tops the scoreboard, and the tarp is spread over left field, ready to cover the infield if needed. Full parking lots indicate a big crowd at the ballpark. (PP.)

A massive crowd is outside Gate No. 4, the main grandstand entrance behind home plate, during the 1960 World Series. Bunting adorns the stadium facade. (PP.)

A mass of fans crowds the lunch counter and a temporary stage featuring Benny Benack and his band. Benack wrote and recorded "Beat 'em Bucs!," which became the anthem of the 1960 Pirates. His Dixieland band was a fixture at Pirates and Steelers games for years, echoing the role of bandleader Danny Nirella in the days of Exposition Park. (PP.)

Perhaps taken after fans headed home, this photograph shows a more serene street scene outside the park. Now, the locals stop for a hot dog or a beer, getting the news and gossip of the day or maybe getting a summary of the game from another fan. Forbes Field was located in a neighborhood, where folks lived in homes directly across the street. (CMOA.)

Bunting everywhere and a packed house suggest this is the 1960 World Series. The box seats extend to the edge of the dugout. The football press box is at center, slung beneath the second deck. The screen behind home is clearly visible. This is Forbes Field at the pinnacle of her 61-year life. (PP.)

One of the most famous photographs in baseball history—Mazeroski launches the ball to win Game No. 7 of the 1960 World Series—also provides an exceptional view of the scoreboard, the Longines clock, and the base of a light tower. (PP.)

By 1965, construction was underway on Pitt's Hillman Library. The exterior of the third base grandstand is seen beyond the construction site. Forbes Field would have to make way for the university's continued expansion. (UP.)

The 1969 season was intended to be the final one for Forbes, and this lovely and nostalgic night view graced the yearbook cover. In the background is the Oakland neighborhood that contributed to the ballpark's vitality but also doomed it with the absence of parking for a fan base increasingly dependent on the car. (PP.)

Construction delays at Three Rivers Stadium forced the Pirates to return to Forbes for the first half of the 1970 season. This aerial photograph appeared on the souvenir program. Gleaming new University of Pittsburgh buildings stand across the street from the third base side. (AC.)

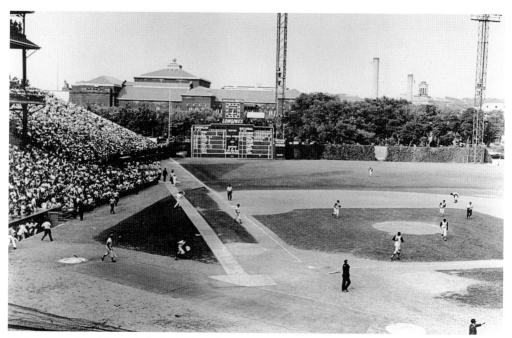

This is how the old gray lady looked at the moment of the last out on June 28, 1970, the putout made by Bill Mazeroski. Over 61 years, Forbes had hosted the Pirates, Homestead Grays, Pitt Panthers, Duquesne Dukes, and Pittsburgh Steelers. It hosted boxing matches, track and field events, fundraising events, and more. (PP.)

After fires on Christmas Eve 1970 and July 17, 1971, the long-delayed demolition began on July 28, 1971. The grandstand was the first priority. The remains of the press box and broadcast booth are seen at top right. (UP.)

The demolition exposed the steel skeleton, including the innovative system of ramps that made it possible to move great crowds over the park's long history. Remnants of the lighting system are stacked on the ground for salvage. (UP.)

The left field bleachers, scoreboard, and outfield walls are all that remain. The great right field pavilion with its towering roof, built in 1925, is gone. The flagpole still stands in deep center field. The sign on the facade still proudly marks the 1960 championship, the high-water mark for the "House of Thrills." (UP.)

Here, the bleachers are succumbing to the wrecking ball. Clearly seen are architectural details in the facade, including the distinctive arches, keystones, and terra-cotta ornament. Today, identifiable fragments of the park can be found in baseball memorabilia auctions, commanding premium prices. (UP.)

The scoreboard still looks ready for a season that will not come. Snow covers the ground, and salvaged sections of stadium seats are lined up. Pitt's Cathedral of Learning looms over the site, which will now give way to the university's long-desired expansion. (UP.)

# MODERN TO RETRO
## THREE RIVERS AND PNC

At the close of World War II, Pittsburgh was at the peak of its industrial might. The region produced 95 million tons of steel to create the tanks, ships, trucks, and weapons that won the war.

But Pittsburgh's reputation as the "Smoky City" did not fit the postwar vision of Pittsburgh's civic leaders. With the dynamic Mayor David Lawrence, the city reformed its government, began to battle water and air pollution, and demolished huge swaths of downtown. The Point was converted from railroad lines to a state park while office towers and high-rise apartments replaced downtown's historic buildings. Soon, neighborhoods from the Lower Hill District to the commercial heart of Allegheny City met the wrecking ball in the name of Urban Renewal.

New highways were built to service the increasingly car-dependent population and its migration from the compact city center to burgeoning suburbs. With its densely built environment and challenging topography, Oakland was a poor candidate for easy highway access for sports venues.

A new stadium was a part of this modern city's vision starting in the late 1940s, but while city leaders explored options, Pittsburgh fell behind in the era of multipurpose concrete bowls. RFK Stadium (Washington, DC, 1961), Shea (New York, 1964), Fulton County (Atlanta, 1965), Busch (St. Louis, 1966), Oakland Coliseum (Oakland, California, 1966), San Diego (1967), and Riverfront (Cincinnati, 1970) all came online before Pittsburgh's new home for the Pirates and Steelers.

When it finally arrived in 1970, the new stadium became home to baseball champions in 1971 and 1979, as well as the Super Bowl champion Steelers of the 1970s and 1980s. What the concrete bowl may have lacked in character, it made up for with the games on the field. But the allure of multipurpose symmetrical stadiums waned, and a new retro-design approach promised a return to the more intimate and quirkier feel of parks like Forbes Field.

After much political wrangling, plans for a new park advanced. Initial designs seemed to mimic Forbes Field but evolved into a unique structure that has been widely hailed as the best of its kind.

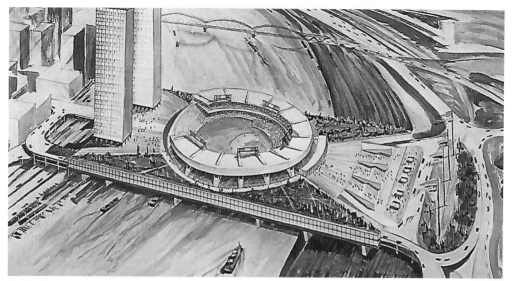

Talk of a new stadium began in 1948. An early and adventurous concept was to build the stadium over the Monongahela River, along with a hotel, marina, and a 100-lane bowling alley. Promoted in this vintage postcard, it failed to gain traction. (AC.)

Mayor Joe Barr, county commissioner Dr. McClelland, and civic leader Edward Magee examine a stadium model in 1961. The design is suitably futuristic and is open-ended at center field. The target site for the new stadium was the north bank of the Allegheny River, where Exposition Park had stood 50 years earlier. Now, the site consisted of rail lines and scrap yards, located directly across from downtown and the Point, which were being transformed into the "Golden Triangle." (PP.)

　　　　　MODERN TO RETRO: THREE RIVERS AND PNC

This rendering places the new stadium, originally referred to as "New Forbes Field," into an idealized site on the Northside. Notably, the only things around the stadium are trees and parking. (PP.)

The sweeping roof and the open-ended design were ultimately rejected. Various reasons have been given, but a symmetrical bowl provided significant cost savings. The circular design was also better suited for football, satisfying the other tenant, the Pittsburgh Steelers. (PP.)

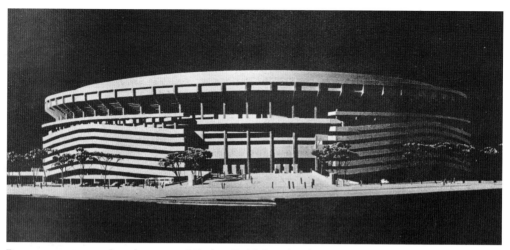

Ramps were integral to the original Forbes Field, but the design of that facade masked much of the ramps. Here, the ramps have become a defining architectural element, dominating the look of the exterior. (PP.)

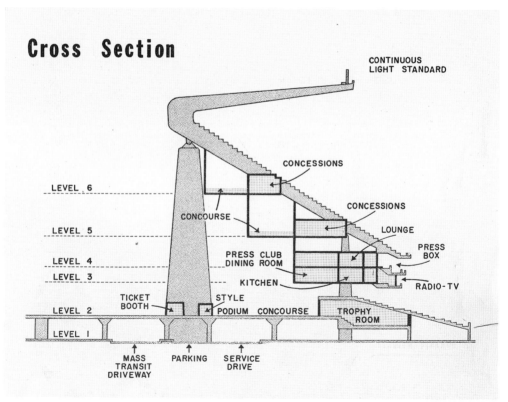

## Cross Section

CONTINUOUS LIGHT STANDARD

CONCESSIONS

LEVEL 6

CONCOURSE

CONCESSIONS

LEVEL 5

LOUNGE

PRESS BOX

PRESS CLUB DINING ROOM

LEVEL 4

LEVEL 3

KITCHEN

RADIO-TV

TICKET BOOTH

STYLE

LEVEL 2

PODIUM CONCOURSE

TROPHY ROOM

LEVEL 1

MASS TRANSIT DRIVEWAY

PARKING

SERVICE DRIVE

This cross section from a 1964 planning document provides a sense of how the interior was to be organized. Continuous concourses would encircle the stadium, and seating would be maximized. (PP.)

This cross-section model illustrates the concept shown in the previous drawing. Transit and support functions are placed below the ground-level plaza and main concourse. (PP.)

These next three sketches appeared in the "Revised Stadium Program," issued by the Stadium Authority on January 9, 1968. The first is an exterior view from the transit level, below grade but not covered by a plaza. Perhaps befitting Pittsburgh, fans now had to cross a "bridge" to reach the turnstiles. (PP.)

This field-level sketch shows the seating bowl with the glass-clad Allegheny Club restaurant at left-center. The cantilevered stadium rim is prominent. (PP.)

Here is a view from inside the Allegheny Club. The club was intended to draw a high-class customer looking for a ballpark experience more refined than rubbing elbows with strangers in the stands. Climate-controlled environs, well-mannered waiters, and menus that did not depend on hot dogs, peanuts, and Cracker Jack were selling points for the affluent fan. Notably, few patrons are showing any interest in the game on the field! (PP.)

Construction of Three Rivers Stadium begins with a ceremonial kick-off by the Steelers venerable owner Art Rooney. Holding the ball is Art's son Dan, later to become US ambassador to Ireland. Art was a lifelong Northsider, living just a few blocks from the stadium site, and Dan would later move into the family house. The surrounding crowd looks to be more old pals of "the Chief" than politicians and corporate bigwigs. (PP.)

Groundbreaking was on August 25, 1968, with a goal of opening for the 1970 baseball season. Here, construction is well underway with the structural elements beginning to define the shape of the bowl. (PP.)

The construction site was highly visible from downtown, just across the Allegheny River. This view in August 1969 may have raised hopes of completion in time for the start of the 1970 season, but labor issues and other factors delayed completion until mid-season. (UP.)

In the spring of 1970, the video scoreboard is being installed. Upper deck seats are partially complete. The target opening was now May 29, but delays in installation of the lighting pushed the inaugural game to July 16. Even then, the stadium opened without parking lots, press boxes, team offices, or the Allegheny Club. Those would take weeks to complete in the summer of 1970. (PP.)

The infield begins to take shape. Originally, Three Rivers had a dirt skin infield around the base paths. A grader is spreading the dirt at third and short. In 1973, the infield was converted to sliding pits at the bases so that the shortstop and second baseman played on turf. In this shot, the movable seats are in their football configuration. For baseball, seats ran parallel to the base lines. (PP.)

The interior nears completion in 1970. The scoreboard, portions of the artificial turf, and much of the seating have been installed. Three Rivers used Tartan Turf until 1983, when it was replaced with Astroturf, which provided a softer base. (PP.)

The Monongahela (bottom) meets the Allegheny (top) at the Point (marked by the fountain) to create the Ohio (left). Three Rivers Stadium was an early effort to reorient the city to its rivers, gradually transforming industrial uses and highways to signature buildings, riverfront trails, and more natural edges, a process that continued with PNC Park. (PP.)

Not sure why the stadium needed a sign—did anyone not recognize this as a stadium?—but a roof-mounted sign was added in 1983. At right is a pedestrian ramp from the Fort Duquesne Bridge, added in 1994 to better connect to downtown. This photograph dates to the 1994 All-Star Game. (PP.)

Pittsburghers love their fireworks, and they are even better if seen from a boat near the Point! The Fort Duquesne Bridge (center) connects downtown to Three Rivers Stadium and the Northside (right). With its riverfront location across from downtown, Three Rivers Stadium was prominent in photographs and postcards, just as Exposition Park was. (PP.)

Several major improvements were made in 1983. The original scoreboard was removed, replaced by added seating and lounge boxes, and a new Diamond Vision board with instant replay capability was installed in the upper deck in center field. Astroturf replaced the original Tartan Turf, and the flagpole was moved to the roof. (PP.)

The Dreyfuss Monument was moved from Forbes Field and relocated to the concourse at Three Rivers. From left to right at the rededication in 1973 are general manager Joe Brown, pitcher Bruce Kison, Fanny Dreyfuss Benswanger (Barney Dreyfuss's daughter and widow of former general manager Bill Benswanger), their son William Jr., and pitcher John Morlan. The monument now stands on the concourse behind home plate at PNC Park. (PP.)

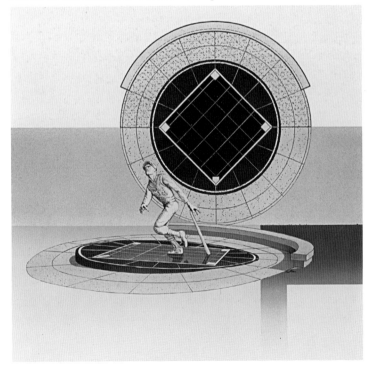

A larger than life statue of Roberto Clemente was unveiled outside Gate B of Three Rivers in 1994. It was later moved to PNC Park, where it stands at the north end of the Clemente Bridge connecting downtown with the Northside. A smaller replica was dedicated in a local park in Newark, New Jersey, in 2012 where a ball field is also named for him. This artist rendering shows the original design for the statue and base. (PP.)

The entrance to the Allegheny Club included original seats from Forbes Field, vintage photographs and plaques, and a World Series trophy. Outside the stadium, Honus Wagner's statue was relocated from its original Oakland location. On the concourse, the team dedicated a bust of former executive Carl Barger after his unexpected death in 1993. (PP.)

The section of Forbes Field's wall where Mazeroski's home run flew into legend was disassembled and reconstructed at the Allegheny Club. When Three Rivers was demolished, the wall was again removed and reconstructed outside of PNC Park, where it now serves as the backdrop to the Mazeroski statue. (PP.)

The entrance to the team office had an impressive display of memorabilia and photographs, including items from the team's early days. It looked like one great man cave. (PP.)

Another display at the team office included jerseys worn by Clemente and Mazeroski, as well as autographed baseballs. (PP.)

The organ room at Three Rivers was on the same level as the broadcast booths, providing the organist with a perfect view of the action on the field, allowing him to react to events and play music to match the moment. In this view from early in the stadium's history, a young Vince Lascheid stands at left. (PP.)

Lascheid was a successful local musician who joined the Pirates as organist in 1970 and played off and on until 2005. His recorded music is still used at PNC Park. This shot, taken sometime after the upper deck tarps were added in 1993 to reduce seating capacity, gives an idea of the view Lascheid enjoyed over his long tenure. (PP.)

By the 1990s, both the Pirates and Steelers wanted new stadiums with new opportunities for revenue, including more lavish luxury boxes. Only 31 years old, Three Rivers was doomed. The scoreboard announces the final series against the Cubs in 2000. (PP.)

After the Pirates fell to the Cubs 10-9 in the final game on October 1, 2000, Pirate great Willie Stargell is shown the statue of him to be erected at the new PNC Park in 2001. "Pops" signals his satisfaction. The glass-front Allegheny Club with its chandeliers is at top right. Stargell was already ill and would pass just hours before PNC's inaugural game. (PP.)

The last game at Three Rivers was a Steeler victory over Washington on December 16, 2000. After that, the process of salvage and deconstruction began. Three Rivers Stadium is seen here from within one of the arches of PNC Park during construction. The 31-year-old stadium was slated to become parking lots. The site now includes the Stage AE music venue and various shops and offices. (PP.)

Three Rivers Stadium was imploded on February 11, 2001, but it took months to clear the debris. PNC Park opened with a Pirates exhibition game on March 31, 2001, and the first official game was held April 9. The location of Three Rivers Stadium's home plate was marked by members of the local SABR chapter and a permanent marker is planned. (PP.)

This early planning model for the new ballpark shows the strong influence of Forbes Field in its arched street-level colonnade, the rectangular second-tier fenestration, and the grandstand roof, but the projecting stair towers spoil the feel. The final version eliminated most of these elements. (PP.)

The design evolved, as seen in this later planning model by stadium architect HOK. The site's prominent location along the Allegheny River and its sweeping view of downtown echoed Exposition Park without the recurrent threats of flooding. (PP.)

Here is PNC Park as it appeared shortly before opening day in 2001, radically different from the planning model. The Honus Wagner statue is not yet in place outside the home plate rotunda. It was installed March 23, 2001. (PP.)

A night view outside the home plate rotunda with the Wagner statue evokes memories of Forbes Field. The ballpark stands just a short walk from the sites of the 1857 game, Recreation Park, Exposition Park, and Three Rivers Stadium in this cradle of Pittsburgh baseball. (PP.)

# DISCOVER THOUSANDS OF LOCAL HISTORY BOOKS
## FEATURING MILLIONS OF VINTAGE IMAGES

Arcadia Publishing, the leading local history publisher in the United States, is committed to making history accessible and meaningful through publishing books that celebrate and preserve the heritage of America's people and places.

Find more books like this at
**www.arcadiapublishing.com**

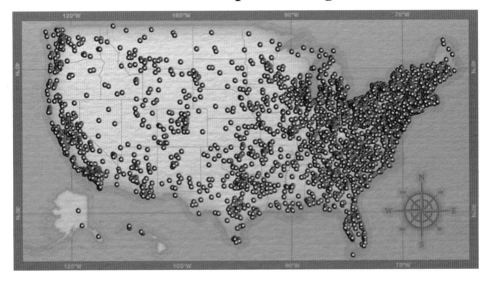

Search for your hometown history, your old stomping grounds, and even your favorite sports team.